STRANGE CREATURES
OF THE SNOW
And Other Great Mysteries

JUST FOR BOYS™ *presents*

STRANGE CREATURES
OF THE SNOW
And Other Great Mysteries

Edward F. Dolan, Jr.

Illustrated with photographs and maps

Original Title: Great Mysteries of the Ice and Snow

DODD, MEAD & COMPANY · New York

PICTURE CREDITS

AP/Wide World Photos, 13, 35, 41, 48, 55, 58, 71, 87, 108.
UPI/Bettman Newsphotos, 20, 31.
Maps by the author, 76, 82, 105, 110.

This book is a presentation of *Just For Boys™,*
Weekly Reader Books. Weekly Reader Books offers
book clubs for children from preschool through high school.
For further information write to: *Weekly Reader Books,*
4343 Equity Drive, Columbus, Ohio 43228.

Published by arrangement with Dodd, Mead & Company.
Just For Boys™ and Weekly Reader are trademarks of
Field Publications.
Printed in the United States of America.

Cover art © 1987 by Field Publications.
Cover illustration by Dick Smolinski.

Library of Congress Cataloging in Publication Data

Dolan, Edward F., date
  Great mysteries of the ice and snow.

  Includes index.
  Summary: Discusses some unusual creatures and events
that have been seen or taken place in cold climates
including sightings of the mysterious Yeti and the
discovery of the remains of a nineteenth-century polar
expedition.
  1. Arctic regions—Discovery and exploration—
Juvenile literature.   2. Northwest Passage—Juvenile
literature.   3. Yeti—Juvenile literature.
4. Curiosities and wonders—Juvenile literature.
[1. Arctic regions—Discovery and exploration.
2. Northwest passage.   3. Yeti.   4. Curiosities and
wonders]   I. Title.
G614.D64   1985   919.8   85-12917
ISBN 0-396-08642-X

Weekly Reader Books offers several exciting
card and activity programs. For information,
write to WEEKLY READER BOOKS, P.O. Box 16636,
Columbus, Ohio 43216.

CONTENTS

Introduction

MYSTERIES EVERYWHERE

The world is filled with mysteries. They are to be found everywhere.

There are mysteries in the air above us. A private plane took off from a Texas airport on a clear summer day in 1950. Carrying five passengers, it flew into the only cloud in sight.

Seconds later, the plane came hurtling out of the cloud. One wing had been ripped away. The fuselage crashed into a field. All aboard were killed.

What had happened to the craft while inside the cloud? Who can say? The incident remains a puzzle to this day.

The sea has produced just as many riddles. One of the most famous concerns the *Mary Celeste*. A graceful two-masted ship, she left New York City in 1872 and headed across the Atlantic. Weeks later, she was found floating near the coast of Portugal. Not a soul was on board. Her crew had disappeared.

There wasn't a sign that anything had gone wrong aboard the ship. Yet the *Mary Celeste*'s entire crew had vanished. They were never found. No one has ever learned what happened to them.

These are two of the best mysteries that the world has ever seen. But there are others just as baffling. They are to be found in the coldest regions ever visited by man—all the misty lands and seas that are covered over with ice and snow.

As we'll soon see, the riddles that have come to us from the ice and snow are many. There is the strange creature that the world calls the Abominable Snowman. Here is a monster that may be animal or man—or perhaps part animal and part man. Who knows?

There are some famous explorers who disappeared when they ventured into the icy wastes of the Arctic Ocean. Three of their number vanished in 1897 when they tried to fly a balloon to the North Pole.

And we'll look at several disappearances that are even more mystifying. They do not concern men who vanished. Rather, they are about ice-coated islands that somehow were not where they were supposed to be.

Most of these puzzles have one thing in common. They are without solutions. No one has ever been able to unlock their secrets. Those secrets may *never* be unlocked.

And so, if you like to be mystified, let's get started. Many a chill down the spine lies ahead.

1

STRANGE CREATURES OF THE SNOW

The man came to a sudden stop as he rounded a curve in the trail above his mountain village. Fear and astonishment filled his eyes. The breath went out of him.

There was a strange creature hunched down on the icy ground about fifty yards ahead. It was feeding on a goat that it had just killed. The creature's body was covered with thick hair. The thing could have been an animal. It could have been a human being. It could have been part animal and part human.

As the man, whose name was Tenzing, gaped, the creature sighted him. The thing straightened, rising to a height of six or seven feet. Its face was wide and flat. Anger flashed in its narrow eyes. With arms flung high, it plunged toward Tenzing.

Tenzing saw that it was clumsy and not able to move very fast. But he waited to see no more. He spun and dashed down the trail to his village. The creature's roar filled his ears, but it faded with every pounding step. Tenzing kept glancing over his shoulder. Each glance told him that the horrible thing was falling farther and farther behind.

On reaching home, Tenzing found the creature nowhere in view. He sank down on a rock and tried to get his breath back. He had never seen such a terrible sight in all his life. But Tenzing knew what it was. He had heard his people talk in frightened whispers about creatures like it for as long as he could remember.

He had seen a Yeti.

The Mysterious Yeti

Tenzing was a member of the Sherpas, a tribal people who live in Nepal. Nepal is a small country located between India on the south and Tibet on the north. For the most part, it is made up of the giant Himalaya Mountains. The Sherpas live high in those mountains.

The Himalaya Mountains of Nepal. Giant Yeti are said to roam high in these mountains while smaller creatures live on the lower slopes.

The Sherpas are a hardy people. They survive by raising a few crops. They also work as guides for the mountain climbers who come from other nations to climb the Himalayas. They lead them up the sides of such mountains as Annapurna and Mount Everest. Everest is the world's highest mountain. Rising 29,000 feet to its snow-covered peak, it looms above the border of Nepal and Tibet.

For long centuries, the Sherpas have told stories of friends and relatives who have sighted the mysterious beings called the Yeti. The stories have been passed from generation to generation. They say that the creatures seem to be a cross between a human being and an animal. Like human beings, they walk upright and swing their arms. But, like animals, they wear no clothing and are covered all over with thick hair. The hair is matted and is most often colored reddish-brown. A few stories say that Yeti with black or gray hair have been sighted.

Each Yeti is said to have a large, dome-shaped head. The dome comes to a point at the very top. Below is an ugly face, with sunken eyes and a wide mouth. The eyes are a blazing red. The mouth is filled with huge teeth. Sometimes, the teeth are sharp fangs.

All the stories describe the hair and face in the same way. But the tales differ when they come to the size of the creatures. Some talk of Yeti that are giants from ten to fifteen feet tall. Others tell of Yeti that are about the size of human beings—from five to eight feel tall. The differences in size have caused the Sherpas to believe that there may be at least two types of Yeti—giants and "little ones."

The giants are said to roam the snows high on the mountains. The smaller Yeti live on the green lower slopes.

Tenzing sighted the Yeti sometime in the 1930s. His story was added to the tales of old. Those tales are many. Some concern Yeti who crept into villages and were seen as they made off with small animals for food. Others whisper of Yeti who broke into houses, grabbed children from their beds, and shambled away into the dark with them. The children never returned.

Many stories tell of Sherpas who heard high-pitched howling sounds while hiking on the mountainsides. Not once did the hikers try to learn the cause of the sounds. They fled in terror, certain that a Yeti was nearby. Other stories have to do with Sherpas who came upon giant footprints in the snow. The sherpas departed—in a hurry.

The various stories have given the Yeti their name. In the Sherpa language, the word *Yeti* has several meanings. Among them are "the creature who lives in the snow," and "the creature who lives among the rocks." The simplest meaning is "the magical one." To the outside world, the strange beings are known by one name—the Abominable Snowman.

But are there really such things as Yeti? No one knows, for sure. All that can be said is that they have puzzled the Sherpas for centuries. Beginning in the late 1800s, people outside Nepal began to hear about them. Since then, the Yeti have become one of the world's greatest mysteries.

Giant Footprints

For centuries, only the people of Nepal knew of the Yeti. Their country is a rugged and primitive one that was little known to outsiders. Only a few people from other nations visited it through the long years. It was not until 1887 that word of the Yeti reached the rest of the world. That word was brought by an Englishman named Lawrence Waddell.

Waddell went to Nepal in 1887 to climb Mount Everest. No mountaineer had ever before managed to reach its 29,000-foot peak and he wanted to be the first to do so. Waddell failed to reach his goal. But as he struggled up the white slopes, he came upon a strange sight—some giant footprints in the snow.

They were, indeed, *giant* prints. Waddell bent over them and found that they measured eighteen inches long. He also saw that

17

they did not seem to be animal paws. Rather, each looked like a human foot. Each had toes rather than claws. There were spaces between the toes, just as there are on a human foot.

When Waddell returned home, he told his friends of his find. With him, they wondered if he had stumbled upon the prints of some animal unknown to science. Or some human who had survived from prehistoric times. Or—a chill went down his spine—some weird creature that was part human and part beast.

In the coming years, other mountaineers tried to win the honor of being the first to conquer Everest. Several of their number came upon odd footprints. Giant tracks were sighted in the 1890s. Englishman John Hunt reported strange footprints in the snow on a 1937 climb. Then, in 1951, another Britisher, Eric Shipton, stumbled upon a line of tracks as he was crossing a glacier.

Shipton's find was an especially important one because he was carrying a camera. He quickly got his camera and gave the world its first photograph of possible Yeti prints. In the picture, they looked exactly like the ones Waddell had described back in 1887. They seemed to be the prints of a giant human—or a creature that was both human and animal.

Beginning in the early 1900s, other stories began to come out of Nepal. They were more fantastic than the ones about the footprints. They were told by mountaineers who claimed to have *seen* the Yeti.

Strange Meetings

The first such story was heard in 1903. William Knight of England reported that he had almost bumped into a frightening something high on the slopes of Everest. Knight said that he had crouched behind a boulder so that the creature wouldn't see him. Then he had watched the thing as it ambled among the rocks.

Knight said that the thing wore no clothing and was covered over with yellowish hair.

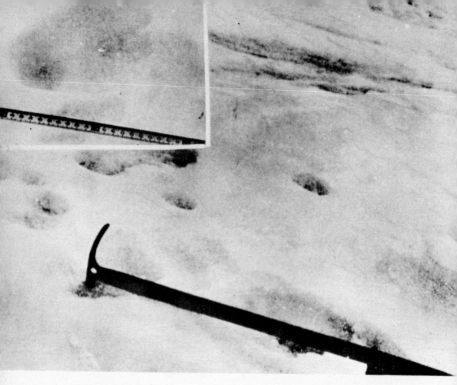

Footprints believed to have been made in the snow by the Abominable Snowman. The photograph was taken during a 1974 search through the Himalayas for the creature.

It had a dome-shaped skull. All the while, the creature walked upright like a human being. In one big hand, it carried what looked like a primitive bow. At last, after five or six minutes, it shambled off and disappeared.

Another sighting was reported in 1923. While hiking up through the snow, a team of climbers glimpsed several dark figures on a slope high above them. The figures appeared to be much larger than human beings. The climbers hurried toward them, only to see them move off. On reaching the spot where the figures had been, the mountaineers found giant footprints in the snow.

Three years later, an Italian climber reported seeing a huge hairy creature that walked upright. It stopped now and again to yank plants from the ground. It would nibble at their roots and then toss them aside. The climber's name was A. N. Tombazi.

The Creatures Attack

The most astonishing of all the stories reached the outside world in 1948. It was told by a team of Norwegian climbers. As they were moving through a high mountain pass in Nepal one day, they suddenly ran into two wild-looking creatures. The things stood upright and were covered with reddish-brown hair. They stared at the Norwegians for a moment. Then they moved toward them. One Norwegian quickly fashioned a loop in his climbing rope and tried to lasso one of the beasts. But he missed. The thing caught hold of him. Its teeth sank into his arm. Then the creature threw him to the ground.

A fellow Norwegian pulled a rifle from his shoulder. He had no wish to kill the creatures. He just wanted to stop their attack. So he aimed the rifle skyward as he fired. The gunshot echoed along the walls of the pass. The creatures fell back in fear. Then they turned and ran. They vanished among the rocks.

A Mystified World

The passing years saw the world's newspapers begin to make front-page stories of the weird things being seen in Nepal. The reports got more and more space as more and more climbers returned with stories of giant footprints and hairy monsters. The news reports were joined by accounts of the old tales told by the Sherpas. The papers then came up with a name for all the creatures—the Abominable Snowman. Today, the term is known in practically every corner of the globe.

The term stirs the imagination. It conjures up pictures of an animal-human with snow clinging to its hair. But, actually, the term is an incorrect one. Not all Yeti, remember, are to be found in the snow. The giants are said to live up in the mountain snow while the smaller Yeti reside down on the green lower slopes.

The term was invented in the early 1950s. By that time, the Abominable Snowman was fascinating people everywhere. They wondered if there were really such things as man-like beings hidden away in the Himalayas. Or were there other explanations for the footprints and the creatures? It was a world-wide mystery. Scientists and explorers knew that there was only one way to solve it.

Expeditions had to be sent to Nepal. They would not go there just to climb the mountains. They would go in search of the hairy beasts.

The expeditions began heading for Nepal in the mid-1950s. The stories of what they found—or did not find—give us our next chapter.

2

IS THERE AN ABOMINABLE SNOWMAN?

Marvelous news reached the world from Nepal in 1953. Mount Everest had at last been conquered. Edmund Hillary, the great explorer from New Zealand, had managed to reach its peak. With him had been his Sherpa guide, Tenzing Norgay.

And there was more news—news that fascinated everyone interested in the Abominable Snowman. During their climb, Hillary and Tenzing Norgay had discovered footprints in the snow. They were giant prints.

Because of their Everest feat, Hillary and Tenzing quickly became two of the most respected men in the world. And so their discovery of the footprints caused the interest in the Snowman to be greater than ever before. It was an interest that triggered many arguments. They raged between the many people who believed in the creature and all those who scoffed at the whole idea.

Arguments, Arguments

The scoffers felt there were simple explanations for all the huge prints and hairy beasts that had been seen. They argued that the prints had been made by animals. The sun had then melted the snow away at the edges of the prints. The prints had grown to the size of a giant's foot.

Next, the disbelievers spoke of the Sherpas who reported seeing the monsters. The Sherpas, they said, were a primitive, superstitious people. Some of their ancestors had once sighted an ordinary mountain animal—most likely, a Himalayan bear or a langur monkey. But they had been blinded by the glare of the snow. The animal had looked strange. Frightened, they had run home with the tale of an awful beast. Ever since, the Sherpas have believed in the Yeti and have let their imaginations run wild. Often, they think they're seeing a Yeti when they're really seeing a bear or langur monkey.

Also, bears are large animals while langur monkeys are smaller. This could account for the Sherpa claim that there are Yeti of different sizes.

And what of the visiting climbers who had "seen" Yeti? They, too, had let their imaginations run wild. Perhaps the thin mountain air had addled their brains. Or perhaps they had heard too many Sherpa tales.

Also, wasn't it possible that some of the climbers had lied? Perhaps they had made up their stories just to get their names in the newspapers.

The people who believed in the Snowman argued back. It was possible that the melting snow had enlarged the prints. But the photograph that Eric Shipton had taken in 1951 showed a print that was not made by an animal paw and its claws. The print had looked like a human foot—a giant's foot.

Finally, all the sightings had been of creatures that walked upright for long minutes at a time. Bears and langur monkeys can get about on their hind legs—but only for a few steps.

As for the visiting climbers, they had all been sensible and courageous men. They simply weren't the types to let their imaginations take over.

Tenzing Norgay, the son of the man who had seen the creature, answered the charge that some climbers may have lied. It was his father who had seen the Yeti on the trail above the family village. Tenzing said that his father *never* lied.

The Search for the Snowman

The people who believed in the snow creatures faced a problem in their arguments.

Eric Shipton had photographed a footprint, yes. But the climbers who had sighted the beasts had never caught them on film. Some of the early climbers had been without cameras. Later climbers said that there hadn't been enough time for picture-taking.

The lack of photographs gave the disbelievers even more reason to say that there was no such thing as an Abominable Snowman.

There was only one way to settle the worldwide argument. Out to Nepal went expeditions to find the Snowman.

The first expedition went in 1954. It was sent by a British newspaper, *The Daily Mail*, and was headed by a reporter named Ralph Izzard. He searched through northern Nepal for several months. All the while, he hoped to photograph a Yeti or—better yet—capture one. No hairy beasts crossed the reporter's path the whole time.

But Izzard did not come home empty-handed. He brought back photographs of numerous giant-sized tracks. And he claimed to have seen the scalp of a Yeti. While high in the mountains, he had come upon it in a Buddhist monastery. It had been shaped like a dome with a pointed top. He said that the Buddhist monks had told him the scalp was more than 300 years old.

To prove his story, Izzard produced several hairs from the scalp. They were given to scientists for study. The mystery of the Snowman deepened. The scientists could not tell what kind of animal the hairs came from.

By the end of the 1950s, three other expeditions had gone looking for the Snowman. Sent out from the United States in 1957, 1958, and 1959, they found several footprints—but nothing else. Not a single snow beast. They brought back plaster casts of the prints for study.

Edmund Hillary watched what was going on through the years. When the expeditions all failed, the conqueror of Mount Everest made a decision. He would lead a search party. Perhaps he would have better luck.

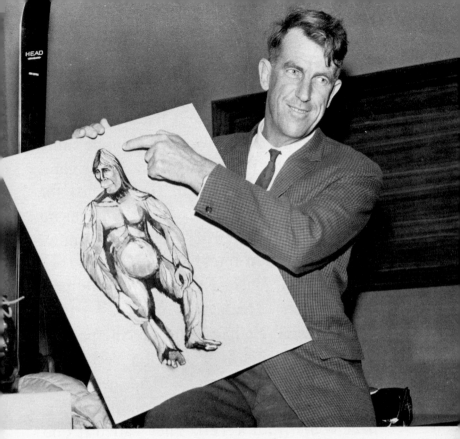

Just before he went in search of the Abominable Snowman in 1960, Edmund Hillary shows a drawing of the creature at a news conference. The drawing was based on descriptions given by people who claimed to have seen the Snowman.

Hillary's Quest

Hillary's quest for the Snowman began in 1960. He traveled high into the mountains of Nepal. At every village, the explorer talked to the Sherpa people and listened to their stories of the Yeti. Now and again, he came upon giant footprints in the snow. He carefully photographed them. He watched for some glimpse of the monsters wherever he hiked. All that greeted his eyes were the snow-covered slopes of the Himalayas.

At last, he reached the mountain village of Khumjung. His search now took a turn for the better. He had heard the Sherpas say that the villagers here owned a Yeti scalp. The Sherpas were right. The people of Khumjung did indeed have a scalp that might have come from a Yeti. They called it one of their greatest treasures and proudly showed it to Hillary.

The scalp amazed Hillary. He had never seen anything quite like it before. It certainly hadn't been taken from a human head. It was much too large for that. Thick hairs, colored black and red, covered the whole thing. It was dome-shaped. The dome came to a point at the top. Hillary knew of no animal with a scalp exactly like this. It fitted exactly all the descriptions given of the Yeti.

The explorer now wanted to do more than Ralph Izzard had done in 1954. Izzard had brought home a few hairs from another scalp. Hillary asked if he could borrow the entire scalp for a time so that all the world could see it.

The villagers liked and trusted Hillary. They knew of his magnificent climb up Mount Everest with Tenzing Norgay. But they shook their heads. They dared not let the scalp leave Khumjung. It meant too much to the village. Hillary might lose it. Or it might be stolen from him.

There was soon a change of mind, however. The villagers agreed to the loan after Hillary explained that he wanted to have scientists check the scalp. It might, he said, help to solve the worldwide mystery of the Snowman. Finally, he promised to donate money to build a school for the children of Khumjung in exchange for the loan.

Hillary immediately traveled to the United

States. The scalp was handed to scientists in Chicago for study. When they were done, it moved on to French scientists at Paris. Hillary impatiently waited for the results of all the studies. Perhaps the worldwide mystery would soon be solved.

What the Scientists Said

At last, the results came through. When he saw them, Hillary felt a keen disappointment. The Snowman remained a mysterious riddle.

The scientists reported that the scalp was very old—perhaps more than three centuries old. But they did not think that it came from some unknown creature. Rather, it had probably once belonged to a Himalayan bear. Or to the dark and long-haired antelope known as the serow. The serow is found in Nepal and other parts of Asia.

The scientists admitted that they couldn't be absolutely certain of their findings. But they felt pretty sure that they were right.

A Sherpa boy poses with what could be the scalp of an Abominable Snowman.

Then they added a puzzling note to their report. They had found parasites in the scalp—tiny organisms that cluster on living things. Parasites cling to and feed on many animals. But they are not found on the Himalayan bear. Nor on the rugged serow.

And so the scalp did nothing but deepen the mystery even more. Had it actually come from an animal? A bear? A serow? Or had it come from *something other* than an animal? From *an Abominable Snowman*?

Still a Mystery

Edmund Hillary returned the scalp to Khumjung. He kept his promise and provided money for a fine school. Though proud of the school, he was still a disappointed man. His search had been in vain. The Snowman was still a mystery.

To this day, the mystery continues. People everywhere wonder if the strange creatures are hidden away somewhere in the

Himalayas. Or if there are such creatures at all.

Should there actually be such beasts as the Abominable Snowman, they do not live only in Nepal. Yeti-type creatures have been sighted in Russia. They've also been glimpsed in North America—most often in western Canada and in the mountainous regions of northern California, Oregon, and Washington.

The Russian Yeti are known as Alma. Having reddish hair and walking upright, they stand over seven feet tall. Many people who have seen the Alma say that the beasts can run as fast as a horse. Others claim to have watched them swim against strong river currents.

The North American Yeti were long ago given two names. In the United States, they are known as Bigfoot. The Canadians call them Sasquatch. *Sasquatch* is an Indian word meaning "hairy giant."

There have been over 300 sightings of the

North American creatures or their footprints since the early 1800s. In 1924, a Canadian lumberjack reported that he had been kidnapped by a Sasquatch family. He said that they had held him prisoner for a week.

Bigfoot and Sasquatch are as mysterious as the Abominable Snowman. If you would like to read more about them, just pay a visit to your school or public library. You'll find many books about both Bigfoot and Sasquatch.

3

THE MYSTERY OF THE *EAGLE*

It's time now to leave the white-capped mountains and their strange creatures. It's time to talk of other mysteries. They are mysteries surrounding the adventurers who first explored one of the world's coldest and wildest areas. They take us far north to the Arctic Ocean.

Into the Freezing Wind

Salomon Andree and his two companions climbed into the *Eagle*'s wicker basket. Above them, the balloon's gasbag pitched from side to side in the wind. The wind was howling north across the ice-covered wastes of the Arctic Ocean. With luck, it would carry the three men to their destination—the North Pole.

Andree looked at the workers clustered about the *Eagle*. They had struggled for days in the bitter cold to assemble and inflate the balloon. But now it was July 11, 1897. The moment for takeoff had arrived. Leaving the workers far behind, he would fly north. If all went well, he would become the first man in history to reach the very top of the world.

The workers heard Andree thank them for their help. Then they saw the 42-year-old Swedish explorer glance skyward at the tossing balloon. He raised his arm. He shouted, "One, two, three. Cut!"

Instantly, knives flashed all about the *Eagle*'s basket. They hacked at the ropes holding the airship to the ground. The ropes

Salomon Andree (the man in profile) is pictured aboard the Eagle *just minutes before the balloon took off on its tragic flight.*

parted. The *Eagle* shot into the air above Dane Island, a speck of rocky land just off the giant island of Spitsbergen. The North Pole lay a little over 800 miles away.

Every man on the ground watched the *Eagle* sweep aloft with its three-man crew and its cargo of supplies—supplies that included dried food, tents, and carrier pigeons for sending messages back to the world. It plunged out over the ice-choked ocean and moved into the distance. Slowly, it became a mere dot on the gray horizon. Then it disappeared from view.

Questions crowded every worker's mind. Would Andree reach the Pole? Would he then be able to turn around and fly back to Dane Island? Or would he sail on to land somewhere on the far side of the world? It all depended on the wind.

As things turned out, the *Eagle* never returned to Dane Island. Nor did anyone ever find it on the far side of the world. The balloon disappeared. Its fate became one of the most baffling mysteries of the world.

The Challenge of the North Pole

In 1897, the North Pole was much like the peak of Mount Everest. It was a place where no one had ever stood. Located in the midst of the Arctic Ocean, it marked the roof of the world. For years, many explorers had yearned to cross the ice that covered the Arctic Ocean so that they could win the honor of being the first to reach the Pole.

So far, all efforts had failed. In 1827, Edward Parry of England had started toward the Pole from Spitsbergen. His men dragged boats behind them so that they could cross the open water that lay between the vast expanses of ice. The boats were equipped with sled runners. But the job of pulling and tugging proved too much for the expedition. Parry had to turn back when 500 miles short of his goal.

In 1879, the American naval officer, George Washington De Long, tried to sail a ship from the Pacific Ocean to the Pole. He entered the Arctic Ocean through the Bering Strait, the narrow waterway that separates North America from Russia. But soon the ice closed round his *Jeannette* and crushed it. De Long and many of his men died of exposure and starvation as they struggled back to civilization.

Next, in 1893, Fridtjof Nansen, the great Norwegian explorer, sailed north in the specially built *Fram*. It was a ship meant not to be crushed when the ice closed in on it. Rather, it was designed to be lifted up onto the white surface. Then, as the ice was pushed along by the ocean current beneath, the *Fram* would ride "piggyback" to the Pole. On entering the Arctic Ocean, Nansen's ship performed as expected. But the ice did not take it to the top of the world.

When 300 miles from the Pole, the current turned south. The ice started to carry the *Fram* back down across the Arctic Ocean to the open waters of the Atlantic. Nansen, however, was determined to reach his goal. Over the side he and a companion went. They headed north with two sledges.

But they met with failure. Bad weather forced them to turn back when they were 200 miles from the Pole. They hiked south, killing seals for food after their supplies ran out. Months later, they came to a group of islands near open water. There they were rescued by a passing ship. It carried them home to Norway. At about the same time, the *Fram* ended her "ride" on the ice. She arrived at the Atlantic and sailed for Norway.

Andree's Plan

Now it was Salomon Andree's turn to head north. But he planned to do the job in a different way. He wouldn't try to push a ship through the ice. He wouldn't try to sledge over the ice. Instead, he would go by air. The age of aviation was dawning. Men were heading aloft in balloons and trying to develop an engine-powered airplane. Andree felt that he was a part of the new age. And so he would become more than the first man to reach the North Pole. He would also become the first man to fly over it.

Andree felt he had every chance for success. First, he was an experienced Arctic explorer. He had worked for ten years in its icy wastes. Second, he was an expert balloonist. Finally, he had picked two fine companions for the trip—Knut Fraenkel and Nils Strindberg. Both were in their twenties. Both were courageous and physically strong. Both were excellent airmen.

But, when the newspapers announced Andree's plan, everyone thought he had lost his mind. The Arctic was a cruel place. It was jammed with humped and jumbled ice. The temperatures often plunged to more than 70 degrees below zero. Vicious winds and storms were a constant threat. A frail balloon couldn't survive in such an area. It would be smashed to bits. Andree, Fraenkel, and Strindberg were going to their deaths.

Vanished

For long days after Andree's departure on July 11, people everywhere waited for news of him. The first word came from a Danish ship that was hunting for seals at the edge of the Arctic Ocean. The captain wired that his ship had been visited by a strange caller just before dawn on July 15. A carrier pigeon flew in and landed on a mast. It brought a message signed by Andree. The message said that all was well aboard the *Eagle* and that the balloon was proceeding north.

The next news was frightening. A Dutch skipper reported seeing something floating on the sea near the Arctic Ocean. The sighting was made on July 17. High waves prevented the captain from drawing near the object. He said it was dark-colored and seemed to be about 150 feet long. He thought it was a dead whale.

But the world wondered if he had seen the *Eagle* and its long ropes stretched out on the

The Eagle *sails away from Dane Island, never to be seen again.*

sea. Had the balloon crashed in the sea after being blown far off course? Had Andree, Fraenkel, and Strindberg drowned?

People everywhere waited throughout July for the *Eagle*'s return. Then August. And then September and October. Heads began to shake. The balloon had vanished into the Arctic wastes and would probably never be seen again. It must have crashed somewhere. If they had survived, Andree and his friends were now struggling to get back to civilization. They would be running out of supplies. They were likely starving and freezing to death. More likely, they were already dead.

Did They See the Eagle?

But what had actually happened to the *Eagle* and its crew? That question gripped the entire world throughout the rest of 1897. It caused so much excitement that people in various places began to "see" the balloon and its crew.

An old woman in Andree's homeland,

Sweden, looked out her bedroom window one night in July. She claimed that a balloon had passed low overhead. There had been a man standing in its wicker basket. No one else in the town glimpsed the airship. The police checked to see if any local balloons were out flying at the time. The answer: No.

A group of Indians in western Canada saw something in the distance that looked like a balloon. They said that it gave off much light as it sailed along. Baffled, people asked how Andree could have been blown several thousand miles off course. Then it was found that the sighting had been made on July 1— ten days before the *Eagle* took off. No one ever learned what the Indians had actually seen. Or if they had only imagined the balloon-like thing.

In August, an Iowa farmer sent a telegram to the Swedish government. It said that the Andree party was lying dead on the northern coast of Greenland. The government authorities wondered how a farmer in the distant United States could possibly know this.

They soon learned. The farmer said that he liked to communicate with the spirit world. Andree and his companions had come to him in a vision and had told him where their bodies were.

Other reports were taken seriously. In September, a fishing ship came upon wreckage floating on the sea near Spitsbergen. The ship could not move in for a close look because of stormy weather. Many people thought the wreckage might be the remains of the *Eagle*.

In November, some Eskimos on the east coast of Greenland heard rifle shots offshore. The newspapers said that perhaps the shots had come from Andree as he and his men had drifted past on an ice floe—a sheet of white that had broken off from the main body of ice.

A Terrible Fact

The various reports were heard until early in 1898. Then they stopped. Throughout the world, people began to accept a terrible fact. Andree, Fraenkel, and Strindberg were surely dead. Perhaps they had been killed in a crash. Perhaps they had been hurt and had died of their injuries. Perhaps they had starved or frozen to death. Perhaps they had fallen through the ice and drowned. Whatever had happened, the vast Arctic had swallowed them.

The fate of the three explorers grew into one of the great mysteries of the ice and snow. However, it was to differ from most of the other puzzles in this book. It would one day be solved.

But its solution would trigger a brand-new mystery.

4

THE ADVENTURE
AT WHITE ISLAND

A Norwegian ship pushed its way through the ice some ninety miles east and slightly north of Spitsbergen. The ship was a research vessel. Its job was to explore the islands in this part of the Arctic Ocean. The year was 1930.

Many great feats had been recorded in polar exploration since the *Eagle*'s disappearance long ago in 1897. On foot and in the air, men had conquered both the North *and* South Poles.

In 1909, America's Admiral Robert Peary had sledged to the North Pole. Then Roald

Amundsen of Norway had become the first man ever to reach the South Pole, which lies deep in the frozen continent of Antarctica. He sledged there in 1911.

Next, two U.S. fliers—Floyd Bennett and naval officer Richard E. Byrd—became the first men to travel to the North Pole by airplane. On May 9, 1926, they took off from Spitsbergen in a Fokker trimotor and returned in fifteen hours.

A mere two days later—on May 11—Roald Amundsen recorded an aviation triumph of his own. Accompanied by Lincoln Ellsworth of the United States and Umberto Nobile of Italy, he took off from Spitsbergen in the dirigible *Norge*. The flight carried Amundsen and his friends to the North Pole. But they did not return to Spitsbergen on reaching their goal. Rather, they flew on and finally landed at the small town of Teller in Alaska. They won the honor of being the first men ever to travel across the Pole and come down at a point far beyond.

The flight also won a special honor for Amundsen. To date, he was the only explorer ever to have reached both the North and South Poles.

And now, as the Norwegian research vessel nosed through the ice, its crewmen knew that still another great feat had just been recorded. A few months ago—in November, 1929—Richard E. Byrd had become the first man to fly over the South Pole. He too, had now visited both Poles.

Roald Amundsen of Norway flew across the North Pole in the dirigible Norge. *The ship is seen here leaving Spitsbergen at the start of its voyage.*

But the crewmen weren't thinking about great feats of exploration today. Their ship had just now come up to White Island, a chunk of land about three miles long and 500 yards wide. After long weeks on the ice-covered sea, the men wanted nothing more than to go ashore and stretch their legs.

The Fateful Walk

Once on the beach, two young sailors decided to walk inland. They came to a small brook. Alongside it lay a cooking pot. The pair thought nothing of the utensil. They agreed that it had been left behind by some other seaman who had once visited the island.

The two men walked a little deeper into the island. They rounded a boulder and came to a stop. Up ahead was a small canvas boat, half-buried in the snow. Its cloth was rotting in the wind. The sailors looked at each other. Someone had sailed that boat to White Island. Someone then hadn't been able to sail it away. Perhaps that stranded someone was still here!

Turning as one, the pair dashed back to their friends on the beach. Immediately, a search of the area around the boat was begun. Within a few minutes, everyone knew that the mystery of the *Eagle*'s disappearance long ago had finally been solved.

Pots and pans were found sticking out of the ice and snow. They bore the words, *Andree's Polar Expedition*. Then several men made a discovery at the base of a nearby rock. They uncovered a body lying in a shallow grave. The grave had been covered over with a mound of stones.

Next, the crewmen came upon a campsite. At its center was a circle of rocks where a tent had once stood. There were shafts of whalebone thrust into the ground at intervals among the rocks. The tent had long since rotted away, but the bones that had been its stakes were still here—as were the rocks that

This could be the remains of Andree's canvas boat. Or it could be what was left of one of his sledges. The wreckage was photographed on White Island in 1930.

had helped to keep it in place.

No one spoke as the men stood looking at the area within the circle. It was covered over with a floor built of driftwood. In the middle of the floor stood a little primus stove. Nearby were several piles of canned goods and a sleeping bag sewn of reindeer skin. Two bodies lay a few feet from the sleeping bag.

Both bodies were well preserved in the bitter cold. Both were wearing woolen shirts and sweaters, heavy trousers, and boots. Both were stretched out in a relaxed fashion and looked as if their owners had just fallen asleep. One body, however, presented an awful sight. Both its legs were almost gone. The crewmen whispered that some visiting bear must have once made a meal here.

Soon, Andree's diary of the *Eagle's* journey was found. At last, after thirty-three years, the world learned of what had happened to the Swedish explorer and his two companions, Fraenkel and Strindberg.

The Flight of the Eagle

The story began with the news that the first hours of the flight had gone well. Throughout July 11, 1897, the wind had swept the *Eagle* steadily northward. But the wind changed direction the next day. The balloon turned west. Then the wind changed again. It blew the *Eagle* southward—over much of the path she had already traveled.

Andree sighed with relief when the wind once more swung northward. But now a new danger appeared. Ice gathered on the balloon's varnished silk fabric and forced her to lose altitude. She was soon whipping along just above the frozen sea. Andree and his men dumped provisions over the side in an attempt to lighten the *Eagle* and give her altitude. The airship refused to rise. The wicker basket hit the surface ice time and again.

The three men fought the problem until a disappointed Andree said it was time to give up. They would never reach the Pole this way. He let the gas out of the great bag. The *Eagle* settled down on the ice. It had been in the air for more than sixty-five hours and had swept back and forth over a distance of 517 miles.

Quickly, the trio loaded their sledges with supplies and headed south toward Spitsbergen. Andree made a promise to himself. On safely arriving home, he would obtain a new balloon and try again. He remained certain that an airship could reach the Pole.

The threesome pulled their sledges southward through the rest of July and then August and September. Whenever they reached open water, they climbed into their canvas boat. They added to their supplies by shooting three bears and six seals. One of the bears was old and had rotting teeth. It tasted awful when cooked.

In early October, tiny White Island came into view.

Death on White Island

Andree, Fraenkel, and Strindberg were in a stretch of open water when they first sighted White Island. They were drifting along on a floe. Other floes crowded the sea around them. The explorers had built an igloo at the center of their floe. They were comfortable and planned to sail on past the island. But they changed their minds just before dawn the next day.

That was when they were jarred awake by a deafening noise. It sounded as if a cannon had gone off outside the igloo. The floe shook along its full length. The trio sat bolt upright as the ice beneath them began to split open. A crack snaked across the floor of the igloo. Sea water gushed up through the crack.

The men hurried outside to find that their floe was breaking up. A part of it lurched away as they watched. Their igloo was left hanging out over the water.

Andree could just see White Island in the dark. The island lay but a short distance away. He knew that winter was closing in fast. It came early in these northern parts. The explorer decided to move to the island's safety. He and his companions would camp there until spring brought good weather. Then they would continue their journey.

In the next hours, the men sped back and forth across the surrounding floes as they transferred their supplies to the rocky hump of land. Often, they had to leap from floe to floe. The ice underfoot was dangerously thin in spots. It promised to give way at any moment and plunge them into the freezing water.

Once everything was safely ashore, the explorers found a sheltered spot for their campsite. They erected a tent. It was fashioned out of the *Eagle*'s varnished silk fabric. They placed rocks all about its base to keep its walls in place during high winds and storms. Driftwood from the beach served as a floor. Into the tent went their bedding, their primus stove, and many of their supplies. They stored the remaining supplies under a canvas sheet outside. Driftwood for fires was piled neatly alongside the canvas "storehouse."

When all was in readiness, Andree and his companions settled down to greet the winter. It was a winter that brought them death on this tiny island a mere ninety miles from where they had begun their North Pole flight.

Strindberg was the first to die. Then, perhaps a few days or a few weeks later, Andree and Fraenkel joined him.

A New Mystery

The deaths of the three explorers brought a new mystery.

How had they died?

Andree's diary of their adventures left no clues. It made no mention of any illness or injury. No reason for Strindberg's death was given.

Several explorers who later saw the diary thought that Strindberg may have drowned. Andree did write of how thin the ice was at the time the supplies were being carried ashore. Perhaps Strindberg had later gone out on the ice to shoot a passing bear, only to have the white surface give way beneath him. It was possible. But there was no way of telling for certain.

An even greater mystery surrounded the deaths of Fraenkel and Andree himself. Again, the record book gave no clue. Not a word of illness or injury. In fact, one paragraph noted that the two men were enjoying a welcome rest after the weeks of struggling across the ice.

All the explorers who saw the diary shook their heads. They could only say what had *not* happened.

Andree and Fraenkel certainly hadn't died of illness or injury. There would have been some mention of being terribly sick or badly hurt.

Nor had they frozen to death. Their bodies were warmly clothed in woolen shirts, sweaters, and heavy trousers. There was ample firewood stacked just a few feet from the tent. And packages of matches in the tent.

But what of starvation? Impossible. Tinned foodstuffs were right at hand by the stove. Still more supplies were piled under the canvas sheet outside.

Finally, there were the positions of the bodies as the crewmen of the Norwegian ship had found them. The bodies were lying in relaxed positions. Everything looked as if

Andree and Fraenkel were stretched out comfortably and talking when death had stolen up on them.

And so what could possibly have happened?

The Norwegian explorer, Vilhjalmur Stefansson, came up with a likely answer.

It centered on the primus stove near the two bodies. It used an oil fuel that gave off poisonous carbon monoxide fumes. The fumes are not harmful outdoors where they can be blown away. But once the stove is lighted in an enclosed area, they are deadly. They have no odor. Their victim has no idea of their presence. He simply becomes drowsy and falls asleep—never to awaken.

Stefansson, who had traveled the Arctic many times, said that the fumes had bothered explorers over the years. Look at what had happened to some of the Eskimos who assisted Robert Peary on his 1909 trek to the North Pole.

At the end of a day's march, they had built an igloo and had crawled inside to heat some water on a primus stove. All of them became dizzy. One fainted and pitched over on his back. When pulled into the fresh air outside, the Eskimos recovered. They said they were going home. They were sure that the god of the north was angry at the Peary expedition for invading his territory. Peary knew better. Carbon monoxide fumes had caused the trouble.

Stefansson believed that those same fumes had taken the lives of Andree and Fraenkel. Here is what he thought had happened.

Andree and Fraenkel had lighted their stove to cook dinner one night. The tent was warm and snug because the rocks that held it down prevented cold, fresh air from coming in. Further, the ground outside was probably covered with winter snow. The white stuff had covered the rocks and had sealed up the tent even more. Finally, the tent was made of varnished silk, a fabric through which air couldn't easily pass. Andree and Fraenkel had stretched out and were chatting as they waited for their food to heat.

As the men talked, the deadly fumes slowly gathered about them. The two explorers had never realized the terrible danger. Quietly, they had fallen into an endless sleep.

Was Stefansson Right?

Is this really what had happened. Stefansson's idea made sense to many people. Not too much was known about carbon monoxide in Andree's day. It was possible that he and Fraenkel were unaware of what its fumes can do.

But no one could say whether Stefansson was correct or not. He had not been in the tent at that terrible moment of death. He was only guessing.

To this day, no one knows exactly what happened there on tiny White Island. The fate of the *Eagle* had remained a mystery for thirty-three years. The fate of Andree and Fraenkel must remain a mystery of the ice and snow for all time to come.

5

WHAT HAPPENED TO ROSS MARVIN?

Andree and his companions are not the only men who suffered mystery deaths in the Arctic. There are several other cases. Here is one of the most puzzling.

Ross Marvin

The date was March 1, 1909. Robert E. Peary of the United States signaled his men to move forward. Their sledges, pulled by dog teams, bounced across the rocky beach. They slid onto the Arctic Ocean's frozen surface. Their destination—the North Pole—lay just over 400 miles away.

Peary, who was 52 years old, had been exploring the Arctic for more than twenty years. In all that time, he had nursed a great ambition. He wanted to be the first man ever to reach the North Pole. He had tried to do so twice—in 1902 and 1906. Both trips had met with failure. Today, he was leaving his base camp on Ellesmere Island for a third journey.

It was a journey that would end in triumph for the explorer. But it would bring tragedy to one of his assistants, a 34-year-old college professor named Ross Marvin.

Though he earned his living as a teacher, Marvin loved to explore. He had accompanied Peary on the 1906 try for the Pole. Now the time had come for another trip. He was among the six Americans and seventeen Eskimos who would drive Peary's sledges and dog teams north.

But, as he hiked out onto the Arctic Ocean ice, Marvin knew that he himself would never

Robert Peary of the United States, the first man to sledge to the North Pole. He never learned whether his assistant, Ross Marvin, had drowned or had been murdered.

reach the Pole. He would be told to turn back before then.

Why? Because Peary didn't plan to take all his assistants clear to the Pole. Their job was to sledge him for part of the distance. He

71

was to ride most of the time so that he could save his strength. As each sledge ran out of supplies, he would send it back to base camp with several men. He would be rested and left with a small party for the last miles to his goal.

The plan was a good one. But it was a disappointing one for Marvin. He was to be one of the men sent back with an empty sledge.

In the meantime, however, Marvin was determined to enjoy the adventure. And a real adventure it proved to be. The temperature plunged to 50 degrees below zero. A howling wind blasted the men as they axed a trail through the jumbled ice. They inched their sledges and dogs up over giant slabs of ice—called hummocks—and slithered down the opposite sides. Often, a sledge broke into pieces at the end of its slide. It had to be unloaded and put back together again. Gloves had to be removed for the job. Bare hands froze after a few seconds in the frigid air.

At times, the expedition crossed ice so thin that it bent dangerously underfoot. Once, it buckled beneath a dog team. The animals dropped into the water. The sledge started in after them. Using all his strength, its driver pulled the rig back to safety. While the explorers were camping in igloos one night, a man walked outside and plunged through the ice. Marvin yanked him out and rushed him to an igloo for a fast change to dry clothing.

An especially bad moment came one night when the men were riding a floe across a stretch of open water. A section broke away and started to drift off with several assistants. They drove their sledges across the gap to safety just before the sheet of ice disappeared into the dark.

Whenever a sledge ran out of supplies, Peary sent it back to the base camp on Ellesmere Island. At last, it came Marvin's turn to head southward. Peary assigned two Eskimos to accompany him. A trip of more than 100 miles faced Marvin. Peary warned him to be careful of thin ice along the way. Then he watched the young man sledge away.

The explorer never saw Marvin again.

Death on the Ice

With five assistants, Peary reached the North Pole on April 6, 1909, and became the first man in history to stand at the roof of the world. He remained there a few hours and then hiked south to Ellesmere Island. The helpers who had returned earlier with empty sledges rushed out to greet him. Only one was missing—Ross Marvin.

It was then that Peary heard the terrible news. Marvin's two Eskimo companions had made the trip safely. But the young explorer had died somewhere along the way.

Peary called the Eskimos to his cabin. With a grim face, he heard the story of the young American's death. The story came mainly from just one of the Eskimos. His name was Kudlooktoo.

Kudlooktoo said that the tragedy had struck

a few days after the Marvin trio left Peary. They had reached an area of thin and broken ice. Marvin had told the Eskimos to rest by the sledge while he scouted ahead for a safe trail. He promised to come back in a few minutes.

But a long hour passed without a sign of Marvin. Kudlooktoo and his fellow Eskimo began to worry. Something had gone wrong. The two went in search of the American. As they walked, they saw broken patches of ice everywhere, with the sea water showing through. One patch brought them to a stop. They stared in horror.

There was a small balloon of fur showing in the water. It was Marvin's caribou-skin jacket. Filled with air, it was keeping his body afloat. The broken ice around the coat told the Eskimos exactly what had happened. Marvin had crashed through. He had fought desperately to get back out. The fight had been in vain. The explorer had frozen to death.

The Eskimos did not touch the body. Their

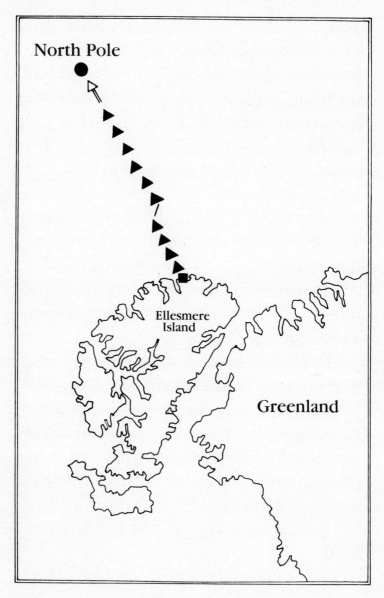

North Pole

Ellesmere
Island

Greenland

people believed that, on dying, a man immediately carried on his work in the spirit world. They were afraid to disturb Marvin and anger the gods of the north. And so they did no more than slip his belongings into the water so that he would not go empty-handed into the hereafter. Then they hurried away.

A Mystery

A saddened Peary returned to the United States. He never forgot Marvin, but he had no reason to think that there was any mystery in the young man's death. Marvin had been traveling in dangerous territory. The threat of death was always present there.

The mystery cropped up some years later. Troubling news reached the outside world from Kudlooktoo's village in Greenland. It said that Kudlooktoo and his fellow Eskimo

Peary's route to the North Pole. Ross Marvin lost his life while traveling south along this path to Peary's base camp.

had made up the story of Marvin's plunge through the ice. Things had not happened that way at all. The Eskimos confessed that they had murdered the American.

Kudlooktoo was reported to be the actual killer. He had grown angry when Marvin had accused the second Eskimo of being lazy. Marvin had threatened to leave the lazy fellow behind on the ice. In a rage, Kudlooktoo had yanked a rifle from his sledge. Marvin had toppled over dead a moment later. The Eskimos had then thrown his body into the water.

For technical reasons, the two Eskimos were never brought to trial. Nor did Peary ever learn of the news. He died in 1920, several years before it was heard. But his men refused to believe the story. They called it nonsense. They said that the two Eskimos must have been insane to tell such a tale.

Peary's men had good reason for this belief. They pointed out that Kudlooktoo and Marvin had become close friends on the hike north. But everyone had seen that Kudlooktoo didn't like his fellow Eskimo. So how could Kudlooktoo bring himself to kill a friend to protect someone he disliked? It made no sense.

Indeed, it made no sense.

But it did add up to a mystery that has never gone away. Did Marvin really fall through the ice? Or was he the victim of murder? There are no answers. There never will be.

6

MYSTERIES OF THE NORTHWEST PASSAGE

If you look at the map of the Arctic, you'll see a group of rugged islands north of Canada. They stretch clear across the length of the country. They make up what is called the Arctic Archipelago. They are lumps of rock and tundra (a treeless, soft soil that is frozen beneath the surface). Surrounding them are waterways that are choked with ice for most of every year. It is to these desolate islands that we turn for our next mysteries.

The islands of the Arctic Archipelago

The Lost Ships

In 1845, Sir John Franklin of England sailed two ships westward across the Altantic Ocean to Baffin Bay. He moved up the bay and swung

82

west into the channel between Baffin and Devon islands. Hours later, he was moving ever deeper into the Arctic Archipelago.

Franklin was searching for what the people of his time called the Northwest Passage. It was a navigable route that everyone hoped ran through the ice-packed waters above Canada to the Pacific Ocean. No one knew if such a route actually existed. But, if it did, it would provide a new waterway for a rich trade with China.

British explorers had been searching for the Northwest Passage for more than two centuries now. Martin Frobisher and John Davis had tried to find it in the 1500s. Edward Parry had made an attempt in 1817. All had failed. Now Sir John Franklin was following in their footsteps.

He, too, was to fail—tragically. The English explorer and his 129 men sailed into the Arctic Archipelago and disappeared. They were never seen again. The question of what had happened to them became a worldwide puzzle in the mid-1800s.

In time, however, that puzzle was partly solved. A number of expeditions went in search of Franklin over the years. Deep into the Archipelago, they came upon some Eskimos who told them that two great ships had once become locked in the ice of a nearby waterway. The ice had crushed one vessel. The other had gone aground on an island. It had broken apart in the crash.

And what of the men aboard the ships? They had shouldered as many supplies as possible. They had started to hike southward toward the Canadian coast. The Eskimos did not know what had ever become of them.

Next, the searchers found a campsite on a small island. The campsite was an old one. Sprinkled about were cooking pots that bore the name of the Franklin expedition. The remains in some of the pots turned the searchers pale. Those remains indicated that Franklin's men were so starving that they had eaten the bodies of their dead companions.

Finally, some Indians on the northern coast

of Canada talked of once seeing a group of tattered white men come ashore from the ice. The whites had made camp there for a few days. Several of their number had died. The others had begun to hike southward into the Canadian forests. There was a rumor among the Indians that some of the hikers had finally settled down with native tribes and had married into them.

In the years since Franklin's disappearance, the Northwest Passage has been located. In fact, two Passages have been found. One runs among the islands of the Archipelago. Roald Amundsen, the discoverer of the South Pole, guided a small ship through it between 1903 and 1906. The second cuts through the Arctic Ocean north of the Archipelago. It was sailed by the giant American oil tanker, *Manhattan*, in 1969.

Neither route is of commercial value today because of all the ice. But many shippers remain hopeful that the route taken by the *Manhattan* can one day be used. Perhaps goods and oil can be shipped beneath it by means of giant nuclear submarines.

Though the Passage has been found, the fate of the Franklin expedition is still a puzzle. Did the starving men behave as cannibals? How many of their number reached the northern shores of Canada? Did some of the survivors finally settle down to live as Indians?

Questions. Questions. But no answers.

The Ship of Ice

It is not exactly correct to say that Roald Amundsen was the first man to sail through the Northwest Passage. The Passage was actually sailed 131 years before Amundsen's trip. It was one of the strangest journeys in history.

For its story, we have to go back to 1775.

In August of that year, a Greenland whaling ship, the *Herald*, ran into a snowstorm near the northern end of Baffin Bay. Giant icebergs crowded the sea. Driven by a hard wind, they began to close around the *Herald*.

Roald Amundsen is recognized as the first man ever to sail through the Northwest Passage. Actually, a strange ship with a strange crew made the same voyage 131 years before his trip.

Her skipper, Captain Warren, could see no more than a few feet through the heavy snowfall. He knew that, at any minute, one of the bergs could crash into his ship and send her to the bottom. There was only one chance for survival. He must swing south and get away from those looming white monsters.

All through the rest of the day and then the night, the *Herald* pushed southward in blinding snow. The storm ended in the small hours of the morning. At dawn, Captain Warren found himself in cold sunlight. He was sailing just to the east of a narrow waterway flowing out of the Archipelago and into Baffin Bay.

There were just a few icebergs in sight. And there was something else. A ship was coming out of that narrow waterway.

Captain Warren put his telescope to his eye. Immediately, he knew that all was not right with the ship. Her sails hung in rags from the spars. Everywhere, long icicles stretched downward from the rigging. Ice coated her rails and hull. It made her glisten from bow to stern in the chilly sunlight. The vessel came slowly toward the *Herald*. Captain Warren could see that the hull timbers were ripped and battered. He told himself that the ice in the waterways of the Archipelago had once tried its best to crush the stranger.

But there was something that Captain Warren could *not* see, no matter how often he swept his telescope along the length of the approaching ship. There was not a sign of life aboard. No sailor was to be seen. Not in the rigging. Not on deck. Not at the ship's wheel.

When the ice-coated ship was quite near, Warren made out her name—*Octavius*. He shouted across the water to her. Perhaps everyone was below decks for some reason. But not a soul appeared in answer to his call. The captain then ordered a ship's boat over the side. He must pay the stranger a visit and find out what was wrong.

With eight of his best men, Captain Warren rowed over to the *Octavius*. They climbed aboard and searched the length of the ice-covered deck. Finding no one, they went below to the crew's quarters. A foul odor hit them as they approached. They opened the door— and stared in silent horror.

Everywhere, sailors lay in bunks and on the decking. They were huddled beneath blankets and mounds of clothing. They seemed to be sleeping, but the visitors knew better. The sailors were all dead, coated over with ice and well preserved in the cold. In all, there were twenty-nine bodies.

Captain Warren turned away and hurried aft to the skipper's cabin. There, he found the master of the *Octavius*. The man, long dead, was seated at his desk. He was leaning forward. His frozen fingers held a pen. The ship's logbook was at his elbow. He looked as if he had been about to write in the book at the time of his death. His body was as well preserved in the cold as those of his crewmen. A greenish mold covered his face. Quietly, Warren removed the logbook from the desk.

Also found in the cabin were the bodies of the captain's wife and ten-year-old son.

Entrusting the logbook to one of his men, Captain Warren returned to the *Herald*. He did not take the *Octavius* in tow because he still faced a long voyage before returning to port. And so he let the ice-covered ship sail on under her ragged canvas until she disappeared over the horizon, never to be seen again.

Then Warren hurried to his cabin to read the death ship's logbook—or what was left of it. During the trip back to the *Herald*, the rotting center section of the book had broken loose and had dropped into the water. No one had been able to retrieve it. Only four pages remained.

But those four pages astonished Captain Warren and gave the sea one of its strangest mysteries. In all, it was a great mystery that contained a number of smaller mysteries.

The Fantastic Voyage

The first three pages told of how the *Octavius*, with a crew of twenty-nine, had set sail from England fourteen years earlier—in the late summer of 1761. She had carried her cargo down around the lower tip of South America and then across the Pacific to China.

The fourth page was right at the end of the book. It was dated more than a year later—November 11, 1762. It reported that the *Octavius* was locked in the ice of the Arctic Ocean near the Alaska coast.

Warren shook his head. How on earth had the *Octavius* gotten *there?* The first pages had indicated that the ship's captain would head home after dropping his cargo in China. But, instead, he had sailed northeast up the Pacific from China to the Bering Strait. He had passed through the Strait and into the Arctic Ocean. There, a short time later, the ice had closed around the *Octavius.* It had brought the ship to a stop and had made her its prisoner.

Why had the captain sailed into the dangerous Arctic Ocean? Had he thought that he might trade with the Eskimos along the Alaska coast? Or had he set out to become famous? Had he tried to locate the North-west Passage by sailing through it from west to east? Or had he some other reason for doing what he did?

Warren would never know. Nor would anyone else.

The first three pages had been written and signed by the captain. But the fourth page was not written in his hand. Someone else had penned it. The words told a terrible story. The ship had now been locked in the ice for seventeen days. The gallery fire had gone out and the captain was trying to rekindle it. His young son had died. His wife was thought to be close to death because she could no longer feel the dreadful cold. Everyone was starving. There was "no relief from the agony."

The page was not signed, and so the strange handwriting added still another mystery to the story. Who had written that fourth page? One of the ship's officers? One of the ordinary seamen?

Captain Warren had long sailed in Arctic

waters. He could easily imagine what had been happening aboard the *Octavius*. More than likely, the crewmen had gone over the side with axes during the first days of their imprisonment. They had tried to chop a path through the ice for the ship. But they had slowly weakened as their food ran out and the awful cold dug deeper and deeper into them. Soon, they could do nothing but lie in their bunks and wait for death.

But no. There *was* something they could have done. They could have shouldered what was left of their supplies. They could have tried to hike across the ice to the Alaska coast. Once there, they might have come across an Eskimo village. But they hadn't done so. Why?

Or perhaps they *had* tried —and had been forced back to the ship in failure. Perhaps the story of that attempt was in the section of the book that had disappeared into the water.

It was one more mystery that would never be solved.

The fourth page ended the written story of the *Octavius*. But there could be no doubt of what had then happened. In time—perhaps within just a few days—death took every life on board. The ice began to carry the battered ship eastward. It dragged her slowly along some route that sent her through the waterways of the Arctic Archipelago. Then, after thirteen long years, it released her. The *Octavius*, her sails torn and her hull glistening in the cold sunlight, drifted into Baffin Bay for her meeting with the *Herald*.

Impossible but True

The *Octavius* and her frozen crew had done what no one had ever done before. And they had done what no one would do for another 131 years. It seemed impossible, but it was true. It had actually happened. A ship with a dead crew had found the Northwest Passage.

But how had the *Octavius* made her astonishing voyage? What had been her exact route? How had she managed to survive for all those years? Why hadn't the vicious ice crushed her? Why hadn't she gone aground and been broken to bits on some island in the Arctic Archipelago?

These questions topped off all the mysteries of the *Octavius*. Captain Warren asked them of himself time and again. They have been asked ever since by anyone who has heard of the fantastic voyage. They will be asked for years to come.

And the answer will always be the same: No one knows.

7

STRANGE ISLANDS

It is baffling when men such as Sir John Franklin and Ross Marvin vanish in the ice and snow. It is more baffling when chunks of land vanish. But that is exactly what some islands in the ice and snow have done. Here are their stories. Let's begin with the puzzler called Dougherty Island.

Captain Swain Finds an Island

It was a gray day in the early 1800s. A cold wind drove the American whaling ship ever deeper into the South Pacific Ocean. The crewmen knew that they had come a long way from home. Captain Swain had just told them that they were far below the southern tip of South America. Very soon, they might see the frozen continent of Antarctica on the horizon.

Suddenly, there was a shout from a sailor at the port rail. "Land ho! Dead ahead!"

The crewmen rushed to his side. They peered into the distance. Yes! There it was— an ice-covered hump that grew larger with each passing moment. At first, the whalers thought they were looking at the shores of Antarctica. But they soon changed their minds. The hump turned itself into a fairly large island.

It was an island that none of them had ever seen before, not in all their years of sailing these waters. Nor had their skipper, Captain Swain. Further, it wasn't to be found on any of his maps.

Swain and his men were not surprised by this. They knew full well how vast the world's oceans were—so vast that they had never been completely mapped. Ships were constantly coming upon small chunks of land that had never before been sighted and charted.

Though not surprised, Captain Swain was deeply interested in the discovery. He wanted to find out what he could about the spot. Then he would warn other skippers so that they would not blunder upon it some night and go aground. Too many good men had lost their lives on uncharted islands over the centuries since ships had first put to sea.

He ordered the helmsman to circle the island. The trip showed the place to be about eight miles long and two or so miles wide. For the most part, its surface was flat and blanketed with ice and snow. At one point, however, a frozen hill loomed to a height of eighty feet. It looked like an iceberg. Seals in the hundreds crowded the shore. Great flocks of birds wheeled overhead.

Now Swain brought out his navigational instruments and tried to establish the island's location. But his instruments were not as accurate as the ones used today. He could come up with only an approximate determination. He found that the island lay about 1,800 miles south and west from the foot of South America.

Into the ship's log went all that the captain learned. Then he sailed away. He had done all that he could. He would now caution his fellow whalers about the place. He had no idea that it would turn out to be one of the world's most mysterious spots.

It was an island that was going to disappear, reappear, and then vanish again.

The Mystery Island

The mystery began in 1831 when the Connecticut captain, Nathaniel B. Palmer, heard about the island and decided to investigate it. Palmer, while on whaling voyages, had spent much time exploring the coast of Antarctica. The continent's giant Palmer Peninsula bore his name.

With his brother, Palmer sailed to the location given by Captain Swain. The explorer spent long days searching the area for miles around—but to no avail. He could see nothing but the vast and empty sea.

Palmer did not think that he had run into a mystery. Rather, he felt certain that Captain Swain had made a mistake in his calculations. The whaler had simply put the island in the wrong place.

Or had he? Eleven years later, another whaler—a British captain named Dougherty—sailed to the location given by Swain. And there the island was! Dougherty ventured to within 300 yards of its shore and wrote of what he saw. His description greatly matched the one written by Swain.

Dougherty, working with improved instruments, fixed the island's location more exactly than Swain had done. This position was some miles distant from the one marked by Swain. But it still seemed close enough for Palmer to have come upon the island while searching the surrounding waters.

And so what had happened? Had Palmer

not ventured far enough in his search? Had he sailed past the island at night? Or had it somehow vanished for a time?

Vanished? That was impossible.

Really? Just wait. Several American, British, and New Zealand whalers sighted the island in the next fifty years. Some wrote of what they saw. Their descriptions were alike—and matched those of Swain and Dougherty. Each mentioned the low shore covered with ice and snow. Each included the hill that looked like an iceberg. In time, the island was named for Captain Dougherty because he had fixed its position so exactly. It found its way into the maps of the world.

Then, in 1894, the American research vessel, *Ruapehu*, set sail to make a study of Dougherty Island. The ship came up to the island's exact location—and found only the empty sea. Quickly, the skipper checked his navigational instruments. Perhaps they weren't working properly and had brought him to the wrong spot. They proved to be in fine condition. He was exactly where he should be. But the island was gone.

During the next fifteen years, the *Rua-pehu* made several voyages in search of Dougherty Island. Not once did the chunk of land put in an appearance. Thinking that it might have sunk beneath the waves, the *Ruapehu* and other ships took soundings of the ocean's depth. The surrounding sea was found to be 2,588 fathoms (15,528 feet) deep.

The men of the *Ruapehu* tried to figure some reason for the island's disappearance. Was it possible that it had sunk to a depth of more than 15,000 feet? Ridiculous! Islands are the visible tops of underwater mountains. The *entire* mountain beneath Dougherty Island couldn't have collapsed!

But perhaps the island had been an iceberg that had finally floated away. That wasn't likely either. An iceberg would not have remained in one spot through the years of its many sightings. It would have been floating hither and yon the whole time. Further, its visitors had all been experienced seamen.

They would have known an iceberg when they saw one.

Or was it possible that Dougherty Island *had never been there in the first place?* Had its visitors been "seeing things?" Again, no. The visitors, remember, had all been experienced sailors—level-headed men. They weren't the types to "see things."

And so what *had* become of Dougherty? Where had it gone? Why had it vanished? To this day, these questions have never been answered. And, to this day, Dougherty Island has never again been sighted. Is it hidden somewhere out in those icy waters? Or somewhere beneath them?

Other Disappearances

Dougherty is not the world's only vanishing island. While sailing near Antarctica in 1739, the French explorer J. B. C. Bouvet de Lozier sighted a small island. He tried to make a landing, but was held back by heavy seas and a screaming wind. The explorer then cir-

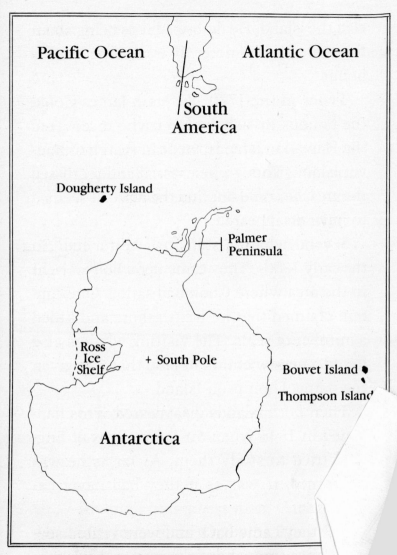

The locations of the vanishing islands of Dou[gherty],
Bouvet, and Thompson

cled the island. He described it as being about five miles in diameter. It was named in his honor.

Twice in the 1770s, Captain James Cook, the famous British explorer who discovered the Hawaiian Islands, went in search of Bouvet Island. Though he crossed and recrossed the area, he could not find the place. It seemed to have disappeared.

Several whaling ships had better luck in the early 1800s. They came upon Bouvet right in the area where Cook had sailed. One captain claimed that he went ashore and killed a number of seals. The visiting whalers also found a nearby chunk of land that was given the name Thompson Island.

Then *both* islands disappeared. This happened in 1846 when Sir James Ross of England tried to study them. As far as he was concerned, it was as if they had never existed.

But they came back and were visited several times throughout the rest of the 1800s. Then, as the twentieth century was dawn ing, Thompson Island by itself decided to vanish. Explorers have visited Bouvet several times in the past years, but Thompson has never been seen again.

Robert Peary's Island

And still other islands could be mentioned. In fact, the history of the sea is filled with the puzzles of disappearing islands. The islands have vanished from both cold and warm areas of the world's oceans.

Though some disappearances remain mysteries to this day, others were long ago solved. America's Robert Peary, the conqueror of the North Pole, played a part in one case that was solved.

In 1906, Peary explored the northern coast of Ellesmere Island. He then used Ellesmere, you'll remember, as a base for his 1909 hike to the North Pole. One day, while studying the Arctic Ocean through his binoculars, he gaped with surprise. There, far to the North, were the low peaks of an island—an island

Though a highly experienced explorer, Robert Peary was fooled into "seeing" an island that wasn't there.

that he had never seen before. Certain that he had made a great discovery, Peary marked the place on his maps and named it Crocker

Land for a friend who was helping to finance his Arctic work.

Peary never had the chance to visit Crocker Land himself. But, in the 1920s, his close friend, Donald MacMillan, led an expedition to the island. He and his companions sledged over the ice to the spot where it should have been. But there wasn't a sign of its low peaks anywhere.

Bewildered, the men traveled back to Ellesmere Island. They hiked to the very shore where Peary had stood when first sighting the vanished island. MacMillan lifted his binoculars to his eyes. He blinked and shook his head. Crocker Land was back in place again! MacMillan later said it stood out so clearly that he would have staked his life on its existence. His men all said the same thing.

But MacMillan knew that Crocker Land did not exist. He realized that Peary had not seen an actual island but a mirage—a trick played on the eyes by atmospheric conditions.

It is a trick that has caused lakes and trees

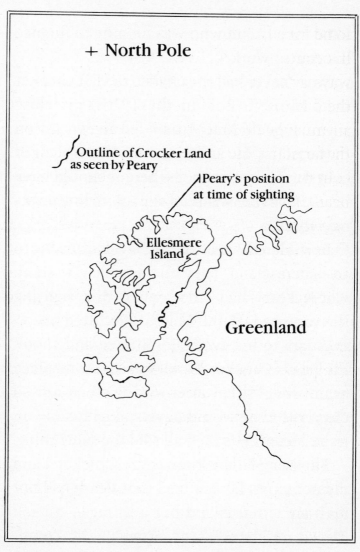

The position of Crocker Land as seen by Robert Peary from the shores of Ellesmere Island

to be "seen" in the middle of barren deserts. It occurs when light rays are bent in odd ways as they pass through layers of air. For the odd bending to take place, the layers of air must be of different thicknesses. Here in the far north, the lower air was a little warmer (a little thicker) than the air higher up. As a result, a large expanse of the ice-covered Arctic Ocean had been made to appear higher than it actually was. It had been turned into an "island."

It was a mirage that had fooled Peary. But it was not a mirage that made the sailors and explorers see Dougherty, Bouvet, and Thompson islands. Mirages are usually seen from a distance. All the men who sighted the three chunks of land had come too close to be fooled.

Those islands of ice and snow remain a mystery as you close this book today. They may always remain a mystery.